AMERICAN BIRD ENGRAVINGS

AMERICAN BIRD ENGRAVINGS

All 103 Plates from <u>American Ornithology</u>

By
ALEXANDER WILSON

With a New Introduction by
DEAN AMADON
American Museum of Natural History, N.Y.

DOVER PUBLICATIONS, INC., NEW YORK

Published in Canada by General Publishing Com-
pany, Ltd., 30 Lesmill Road, Don Mills, Toronto,
Ontario.
Published in the United Kingdom by Constable
and Company, Ltd., 10 Orange Street, London
WC 2.

American Bird Engravings, first published by
Dover Publications, Inc., in 1975, contains all the
plates from *American Ornithology; or, The Natural History of the Birds of the United States.
Plates Engraved and Colored from Original Drawings Taken from Nature. By Alexander Wilson;*
and Supplement, as published by Porter & Coates,
Philadelphia, n.d. (ca. 1871). See Bibliographical
Note for further details.

The complete set of 103 plates appears in black
and white in this edition, although some of the
originals used were in color. In addition, eight
plates are repeated here in full color.

New features, prepared specially for the present
edition, are: an Introduction by Dean Amadon,
a Bibliographical Note and an Index of Birds Illustrated giving modern common and scientific
names.

International Standard Book Number: 0-486-23195-X
Library of Congress Catalog Card Number: 75-9180

Manufactured in the United States of America
Dover Publications, Inc.
180 Varick Street
New York, N.Y. 10014

ALEXANDER WILSON, 1766~1813

An Appreciation by Dean Amadon

In 1966, on a motor trip to Scotland, we drove through the town of Paisley, and our hosts commented on the shawls for which that mill town is, or was, famous. "Wait," I said, as we passed a small park, "there is a statue of a man with a bird in his hand." It was Alexander Wilson, "Father of American Ornithology," honored in 1867 by the town in Scotland where he was jailed as a youth for a scathing poem "The Shark," deriding a local mill owner. An exile to America, Wilson never returned to Scotland.

Yet his childhood and young manhood in Scotland had laid the foundations for his future career. He had first learned to discriminate and appreciate birds while skulking around Scottish estates as a poacher. He had published two or three slender volumes of verse, gaining facility as a writer. After ten confining years as a weaver, he had become a wandering peddler—perhaps we could say traveling salesman—of the woolens produced by his native region. This had trained him for the long journeys on foot that he was to undertake in America.

After reaching these shores in 1794, Wilson was obliged to support himself in various, often menial ways. At times he taught school, but at others he had to take up his old hated trade of weaver, or again he was temporarily an itinerant peddler. Indeed, in one sense he remained a peddler for life, but in later years he hawked his own ornithological masterpiece, one of the ornaments of the cultural life of the period.

Wilson's latent interest in natural history was stimulated when he visited Bartram's Garden in Philadelphia in 1802 and was befriended by the gifted author of *The Travels of William Bartram*. Soon Wilson was trying his hand at painting birds, and, encouraged by Bartram, formulated his ambitious plan for a multivolume work on American birds.

Once Wilson was fairly launched on his task, it became almost an obsession with him. And indeed almost Herculean labors were involved: not merely the field work—finding, observing, collecting, painting and describing the birds—but the endless tasks of pushing the production, supervising the plates and getting subscribers (who refused to put up a red cent until they had one volume of the publication in hand).

The field work and the visits to various districts east of the Mississippi in search of subscribers to the publication could in some measure be combined. With the first volume of the *American Ornithology* under one arm; gun in hand, should he encounter new birds during the long intervals when he was obliged to walk, for lack of stagecoach fare; Wilson remained on the move. He was usually received courteously, but was often bitterly disappointed at failure to secure subscriptions. After all, $100 was a big commitment in those days, and even institutions such as Princeton or Rutgers were unwilling to subscribe, much less the faculty members, themselves often earning only a scanty living.

Then Wilson's luck would change. In New York an heiress who had recently married the celebrated Professor Samuel Latham Mitchill of Columbia University surprised Wilson by saying that she was a keen admirer of his verse. He was invited to the Mitchill home, where, according to a contemporary account, "The doctor poured out the immense treasures of his prompt memory; and gave ingenious illustrations on diverse topics for [Wilson's] mental gratification." A greater gratification to the hard-pressed naturalist was the favorable review Mitchill wrote of Wilson's work, and praise from DeWitt Clinton and others. A number of subscriptions were received.

Wilson, shy and retiring, often rebuffed efforts at friendship; yet he did meet important people. To be sure, he had nothing to do with the fact that he was christened by a Reverend Witherspoon who, within the year, departed for the New World, became principal of an academy that eventually became Princeton University and later was the only clergyman to sign the Declaration of Independence! In later life, though, it was Wilson's tireless quest both for birds and for subscribers to his work that led him to correspond with and later meet outstanding individuals, including even President Jefferson. The latter unintentionally sent Wilson on a wild chase for an elusive treetop songster. The eventual conclusion was that it was a

Towhee, a shrubland bird that does ascend into the trees to sing, but scarcely with the sweet melody Jefferson attributed to it.

Wilson gravitated to perplexed men like himself; among them was Meriwether Lewis of Lewis and Clark Expedition fame. The explorer turned over to Wilson two or three new western birds to describe. Later Wilson visited Lewis' lonely grave near Natchez, interviewed the wild couple who had reported his death, and concluded that they had probably murdered the explorer but reported it to be a suicide. Characteristically, Wilson wrote this up and gave copies of his article to a few individuals, but discouraged publication.

It was quite by accident, too, that Wilson met Audubon, then engaged in one of his ill-fated business ventures, this time in Louisville, Kentucky. Audubon was years younger, still in his twenties, and of a sanguine personality; one would not have expected the two men to hit it off and they did not. It was a crushing blow for Wilson to find an unknown frontiersman whose paintings were superior to his own. Audubon, writing of the encounter years later, gave a rather self-serving version of why he did not subscribe to Wilson's work; probably the true reason was poverty! But in fairness to Audubon, he did take his visitor on a bird-watching trip, if we may call it that, through the countryside.

Wilson's relations with women are not clearly defined in any of the literature I have scanned. His early troubles in Scotland are supposed to have been aggravated by his familiarities with a disreputable local lass. A few years after reaching our shores he fled Milestown, Pennsylvania, where he had been teaching, forgetting his trunk of personal belongings and even his coat; possibly he had had the misfortune to fall in love with a married woman. In any event, he dismissed Milestown as "a settlement of canting, preaching, praying, snivelling, ignorant Presbyterians."

Considering all his travels, efforts and disappointments, it is no wonder that Wilson was worn out at the age of 47. He died of exposure and fever following a field trip, but would have recovered had he been in better physical condition. Wilson's early demise, and his withdrawn and taciturn nature, might convey the impression that he was never robust. This cannot have been the case. Ten years after coming to America, he went on a trip by foot, with a cousin and another young man, from the environs of Philadelphia to Niagara Falls. Most of the way, hundreds of miles, was virtual wilderness; here and there, along rivers and lakes, there were crude clearings and settlements. Wilson would romp ahead or lag behind, observing, shooting game for food, reflecting. On his return he wrote a long narrative poem, "The Foresters," which was published. Surely this was not the life style of a hopeless introvert or hypochondriac.

Wilson is often called the "Father of American Ornithology" but it would be wrong to assume from this that most of the hundreds of species of American birds, and especially those of the East, were still awaiting discovery. The tenth edition of Linnaeus' *Systema Naturae,* which appeared in 1758, attempted to name and briefly describe all known species of birds and other animals, and already contained the more conspicuous American species. Linnaeus had never seen a specimen of many of these, but had taken his descriptions from earlier published accounts. Of the latter, the most notable was the folio, with color plates, by Mark Catesby titled *Natural History of Virginia, Carolina, and the Bahama Islands,* which appeared in 1731. Catesby, though a botanist, painted about 175 species of American birds; Linnaeus had the later pleasure of naming them scientifically, and so the source is now cited as "ex Catesby." The historian of ornithology Elsa G. Allen calls Catesby the "Founder" of American ornithology, Wilson the "Father."

Of course, after Catesby there were still numerous scarcer or more furtive species to be discovered, described and named. Outstanding examples are that colorful and uniquely American group, the wood warblers, of which as many as 25 species can be found in a single spring day in the eastern woodlands.

Of the 38 species of eastern warblers, no fewer than thirteen were named scientifically for the first time by Linnaeus and another six by Gmelin, his successor in compiling the *Systema Naturae.* Six others were described by other older ornithologists or compilers. For example, that gem of the family, the Blackburnian Warbler, was given its first Latin name by one P. L. S. Müller in the year of American independence, from a winter migrant sent to Europe from French Guiana in South America. At the other geographical extreme, the Blackpoll Warbler was named as early as 1772 from a specimen from Ft. Severn, Hudson Bay. Thus, the cream of the crop was already known to science by the time the "Father of American Ornithology" came along. It is a tribute to Wilson's industry and powers of discrimination, however, that he found and described no fewer than an additional ten species of warblers. Most of them are rather obscure species, but they include two gems, the Magnolia and the Bay-breasted Warblers. Little remained undiscovered among the eastern species of the warbler family after Wilson's work. Audubon named two species, the rare and local Bachman's Warbler, now perhaps extinct, and Swainson's Warbler, another furtive species.

What about Wilson as an artist? The books had to be illustrated, there was no one else to do it. Wilson had little or no training as an artist and no inherent gift of draughtsmanship. But he worked very hard at it and the results are often quite good and occasionally laudable, especially the paintings of the larger birds, such as the Snowy Owl or the Whip-poor-will. At one time or another during the difficult and expensive undertaking, Wilson did everything—the painting, the etching of the copper plate, the impression, and finally the hand coloring of the plate. Most of the etching and color work, however, was done by the printer Alexander Lawson and his assistants.

In judging Wilson's art one must also recall that representations of birds up to that time had been stiff and unlifelike. Audubon was to change this with a vengeance, indeed going too far in the other direction, but Audubon came later, and Wilson had only the one brief look at his work, there in distant Louisville.

Like Audubon, Wilson made much use of the collecting gun. After he began serious study of birds in America he could make little progress without specimens before him to draw and compare. Cruising off the New Jersey coast, he is said to have shot 25 of the little migratory storm petrels, or Mother Carey's Chickens, before obtaining one intact enough to serve as a model for a painting.

Without any financial resources whatever, Wilson performed a miracle in getting his multivolume and relatively expensive *American Ornithology* under way. He could not, with rare exceptions, afford the luxury of devoting an entire plate to a single species. Unfortunately some of his more striking paintings of large birds have less attractive diminutive species tucked in here and there around the corners.

George Ord, who completed the *American Ornithology,* was a wealthy dilettante, inspired as much by a cordial dislike of the young upstart Audubon as by admiration of Wilson. Still, it is fortunate for Wilson's reputation that Ord did appear on the scene late in the Scotsman's life. Like others Ord judged from Wilson's writing and painting that he must be in comfortable circumstances, a man who relaxed, when evening came, in a well-stocked library. Ord may have been surprised that he was never invited to the ornithologist's home, but probably thought this was because he was a bachelor. Actually, Wilson was living from hand to mouth as a boarder; the few shekels he came by went into his lifework. He had virtually no library, and the quotations in his writings came from memory or from notes made during occasional visits to centers of learning or to better-endowed homes.

After Wilson's death, Ord was dismayed to find almost nothing in the way of manuscript or field notes among his meager effects. Fortunately for posterity, Ord was the type to proceed blandly, and as a result the world has Wilson, Alexander, *American Ornithology,* nine volumes, completed, and not an unfinished symphony.

Although it has often been implied that Wilson's reputation and work were neglected, this was only by comparison with the fame that came to Audubon. By most standards, Wilson did receive posthumous recognition, for whatever that is worth. Zimmer, in his bibliography of fine ornithological books, required several pages to list and describe later editions of *American Ornithology.* One of these contains a lengthy biography and appreciation of Wilson by George Ord. Sir William Jardine did the same for another edition.

Thus Wilson was not forgotten. One of the best-known American ornithological societies bears his name, as do several species of birds, including the Wilson's Phalarope and Wilson's Warbler.

Of even the greatest scientists, it may usually be said that if they had not made their discoveries and insights, someone else, before long, would have done so. If Wilson had not written of American birds and described many of them, the pleasure would have fallen to another. But at that time and place he was the only individual with the intense drive to bring such a publication to completion, and thus to stimulate later work, both scientific and popular, on American natural history. As Elliott Coues said, if all pre-Wilsonian literature on American birds had been destroyed it would not have been a loss, but a blessing. Quite apart from his great masterpiece, however, this complex and often starcrossed man who despite many adversities, within and without, succeeded in his great goal, will continue to intrigue students of the human condition.

Surely we cannot conclude without a sample of Wilson's prose and poetry. The following is from his account of the Osprey, or Fish-Hawk, and includes some verse in the style of Oliver Goldsmith:

The flight of the Fish-Hawk, his manœuvres while in search of fish, and his manner of seizing his prey, are deserving of particular notice. In leaving the nest he usually flies direct till he comes to the sea, then sails around in easy curving lines, turning sometimes in the air as on a pivot, apparently without the least exertion, rarely moving the wings, his legs extended in a straight line behind, and his remarkable length and curvature or bend of wing, distinguishing him from all other Hawks. The height at which he thus elegantly glides is various, from one hundred to one hundred and fifty, and two hundred feet, sometimes much higher, all the while calmly reconnoitering the face of the deep below. Suddenly he is seen to check his course, as if struck by a particular object, which he seems to survey for a few moments with such steadiness that he appears fixed in air, flapping his wings. The object however he abandons, or rather the fish he had in his eye has disappeared, and he is again seen sailing around as before. Now his attention is again arrested, and he descends with great rapidity; but ere he reaches the surface, shoots off on another course, as if ashamed that a second victim had escaped him. He now sails at a short height above the surface, and by a zig-zag descent and without seeming to dip his feet in the water, seizes a fish, which after carrying a short distance, he probably drops, or yields up to the Bald Eagle, and again ascends by easy spiral circles, to the higher regions of the air, where he glides about in all the ease and majesty of his species. At once from this sublime aerial height he descends like a perpendicular torrent, plunging into the sea with a loud rushing sound, and with the certainty of a rifle. In a few moments he emerges, bearing in his claws his struggling prey, which he always carries head foremost; and having risen a few feet above the surface, shakes himself as a water spaniel would do, and directs his heavy and laborious course directly for the land.

If the wind blow hard, and his nest lie in the quarter
from whence it comes, it is amusing to observe with
what judgment and exertion he beats to windward, not
in a direct line, that is, *in the wind's eye,* but making
several successive tacks to gain his purpose . . . .

> Soon as the Sun, great ruler of the year!
> Bends to our northern climes his bright career;
> And from the caves of ocean calls from sleep
> The finny shoals and myriads of the deep;
> When freezing tempests back to Greenland ride;
> And day and night the equal hours divide;
> True to the season, o'er our sea-beat shore,
> The sailing Osprey high is seen to soar,
> With broad unmoving wing; and, circling slow,
> Marks each loose straggler in the deep below:

> Sweeps down like lightning! plunges with a roar!
> And bears his struggling victim to the shore.

Those desiring more information about Wilson may consult the rather lengthy account with which Elsa G. Allen concludes her *History of American Ornithology Before Audubon,* published by the American Philosophical Society in 1951. Ten years later Robert Cantwell's sumptuous, well-illustrated and in many respects definitive biography, *Alexander Wilson: Naturalist and Pioneer,* reached the presses. Cantwell, unfortunately, knew little about birds, and thus was unable to set Wilson's contributions to ornithology in their context. But in all other respects his biography is a most complete account of the poet and naturalist.

BIBLIOGRAPHICAL NOTE

The first edition of Alexander Wilson's *American Ornithology* appeared in nine volumes between 1808 and 1814 and was published by Bradford and Inskeep of Philadelphia.

Wilson had succeeded in interesting these publishers in his project while he was doing some editorial work for them in 1807. Once the work was under the aegis of a reputable firm, the noted engraver Alexander Lawson, who several years before had declined his friend Wilson's private invitation to engrave, took on the task of preparing the drawings for the printer. Even so, Lawson ended up working for a dollar a day because Wilson's project was throughout beset by financial difficulties.

Lawson did about two thirds of the engraving alone. John G. Warnicke, an established general engraver, was responsible for twenty plates; George Murray, usually a banknote engraver, and Benjamin Tanner, later involved in banknotes but still general at this time, were responsible for four and one, respectively.

The engravers were never free from the indefatigable and energetic superintendence of Wilson. They worked from drawings which Wilson had sketched directly from nature, and the ornithologist was often able to supply them with freshly killed specimens so they could better reproduce and improve his original (often stilted) productions. After the engravers had finished a plate, Wilson colored it—again using a freshly killed bird as a model wherever possible. Wilson complained that his onerous coloring job kept him from devoting enough time to gathering information in the field. He eventually found some assistants, but was dissatisfied with their clumsy efforts and expended more time than before in supervising them. From first to last, the coloring was Wilson's bane—though it was his only means of monetary support while *American Ornithology* was in press.

Wilson died in 1813 with the first seven volumes of his *Ornithology* in print. The work was completed by George Ord, a rich admirer of Wilson's and a friend of the ornithologist's during his last years. In the preface to Volume Eight, which came out in 1814, Ord states that Wilson had completed the text and had superintended all but one of the engravings for that volume. For Volume Nine, however, Wilson had completed material for only three plates, and his notes for the text were scanty. Ord wrote the text, supplementing Wilson's notes with his own observations. The publishers and engravers decided to remove Wilson's drawing of the Great-Footed Hawk from a sketch containing several birds and engrave it as a separate plate. Still, Volume Nine contains only four plates as compared with the eight or nine in each of the other eight volumes. Ord wrote a sketch of Wilson's life which occupies the extra space in this volume.

Amercan Ornithology contains 76 plates in all and covers well over 250 birds. The birds are not arranged in systematic sequence of species, since Wilson was constantly in the process of gathering material and thought it more practicable to draw and write in the same order in which he found. The text consists of essays, each running roughly to a length of some four to five large-type quarto pages. At the head of each essay, Wilson places the bird under discussion in its scientific class. He precisely details its physical features, and expatiates on its habits and characteristics in a somewhat rhapsodic style. The essays are not unlike those that Audubon was later to write.

In 1824-5, Ord published a revised edition of the last three volumes of *American Ornithology*. He changed some of the Latin nomenclature, altered parts of the text, and added some new matter. The life of Wilson he greatly expanded, adducing many of the ornithologist's letters to support and fill out his account.

Also in 1824-5, Charles Lucien Bonaparte, Prince of Canino, a member of the famous Corsican family and later a participant in the Italian movement for independence, wrote five essays discussing Wilson's Latin nomenclature for the *Journal* of the Academy of Natural Sciences of Philadelphia. He followed these up by publishing in four volumes (Carey, Lea & Carey, Philadelphia; London, John Miller; 1825-33) a supplement to Wilson entitled *American Ornithology; or the Natural History of Birds inhabiting the United States, not given by Wilson*. Bonaparte wrote more easily in Italian or French than he did in English, so the text of his work is somewhat stilted compared with Wilson's outpourings. Bonaparte also boasted no artistic skills, but he succeeded, as the preface to Volume One states, "through the happy pencil of Mr. Titian Peale," one of the many artistic sons, all named after great Renaissance masters or Philadelphia heroes, of Charles Willson Peale, the famous portrait and miniature painter, museum proprietor, scientist, and inventor. Titian Peale had explored bird life as far west as the Rocky Mountains on an expedition led by Major Long in 1819. The plates in Volume One of Bonaparte's work represent the sketches Peale did on this western expedition. Peale was sent to Florida by the publishers to gather material for the succeeding volumes. Alexander Lawson did the engraving for the 27 plates that accompanied the four volumes. Alexander Rider, another established artist, was enlisted to do all of the coloring. In addition, Rider helped Peale with some of the initial sketches, working always from "the recent bird, and not from the preserved specimen." A single plate—that depicting the Great Crow Blackbird —was drawn from nature by Rider assisted by John James Audubon.

The popularity of *American Ornithology* in the nineteenth century is indicated by the great number of editions that came out. Among these were several English and Scottish editions published mostly during the 1830's and 40's. In 1828-9, Collins & Co. of New York published a full edition of Wilson, embodying in three octavo volumes the revised Ord text of 1824-5 together with many new notes which Ord prepared specially for this edition. The plates were published separately in a handsome large quarto volume. This general format was also followed by Porter & Coates of Philadelphia when they issued a combined edition of Wilson and Bonaparte in 1871. Three octavo volumes contain the texts of both men—using, again, the updated Ord text of Wilson. Two large quarto volumes contain the plates—the first volume containing Wilson's 76 plates and the second, Bonaparte's 27. The publication date does not appear in any of the five volumes. It is almost certainly from a set of these two volumes—or perhaps from a largely uncolored printing which Porter & Coates made from the engravings used in preparing their edition—that the present Dover edition of the plates has been reproduced.

AMERICAN BIRD ENGRAVINGS

1. *Corvus cristatus*, Blue Jay. 2. *Fringilla Tristis*, Yellow-Bird or Goldfinch.

3. *Oriolus Baltimorus*, Baltimore Bird.

Drawn from Nature by A. Wilson.

Engravd by A. Lawson.

1. *Turdus Melodus*, Wood Thrush. 2. *Turdus Migratorius*, Red-breasted Thrush, or Robin

3. *Sitta Carolinensis*, White breasted black-capped Nuthatch. 4. *Sitta Varia*, Red-bellied-black-capped Nuthatch.

1. *Picus Auratus*. Gold-winged Woodpecker. 2. *Emberiza Americana*. Black-throated Bunting.

3 *Motacilla Sialis*. Blue Bird.

Drawn from Nature by A. Wilson.

3

Engraved by G. Murray.

Oriolus Spurius, Orchard Oriole. 1. *Female*. 2. *and* 3. *Males of the second and third years.*
4. *Male in complete plumage.* a. *Egg of the* Orchard Oriole. b. *Egg of the* Baltimore Oriole.

Drawn from Nature by A Wilson.   Engrav'd by Hicson.

Drawn from nature by A. Wilson. *Engraved by A. Lawson.*

1. Great American Shrike, or Butcher Bird. 2. Pine Grossbeak. 3. Ruby-crown'd Wren. 4. Shore Lark.

5

Drawn from Nature by A. Wilson.

Engraved by A. Lawson.

1. Maryland Yellow-throat. 2. Yellow-breasted Chat. 3. Summer Red Bird. 4. Female. 5. Indigo Bird. 6. American Redstart.

1. *Cedar Bird.* 2. *Redbellied Woodpecker.* 3. *Yellow-throated Flycatcher.* 4. *Purple Finch.*

Drawn from Nature by A. Wilson.

7

Engraved by G. Murray

1,Brown Creeper. 2.Golden-crested Wren. 3.House Wren. 4.Black-capt Titmouse. 5.Crested Titmouse. 6.Winter Wren.

Drawn from Nature by A.Wilson.

Engraved by A.Lawson.

1. Red-headed Woodpecker. 2. Yellow-bellied W. 3. Hairy W. 4. Downy W.

9

Drawn from Nature by A. Wilson.

Engraved by A. Lawson.

1. Mocking Bird. 2. Egg. 3 & 4. Male and Female Humming Bird, nest and eggs. 5. Towhé Bunting. 6. Egg.

Drawn from Nature by A.Wilson. 1. Cardinal Grosbeak. 2. Female & egg. 3. Red Tanager. 4. Female & egg. Engraved by A.Lawson.

Drawn from Nature by A.Wilson.

Engraved by A.Lawson.

1, Rice Bunting. 2. Female. 3. Red-eyed Flycatcher. 4. Marsh Wren. 5. Great Carolina Wren. 6. Yellow-throat Warbler.

12

1, Tyrant Flycatcher. 2, Great Crested F. 3, Small green Crested F.
4, Pewee F. 5, Wood Pewee F.

Drawn from nature by A.Wilson.

Engraved by A.Lawson.

13

Drawn from Nature by A.Wilson.   *Engraved by A.Lawson.*

1 Brown Thrush. 2 Golden-Crowned Th. 3 Cat Bird. 4 Bay-breasted Warbler. 5 Chesnut-sided W. 6 Mourning W.

1. Red-cockaded Woodpecker 2. Brown-headed Nuthatch 3. Pigeon Hawk 4. Blue-winged Yellow Warbler 5. Golden-winged W. 6. Blue-eyed Yellow W. 7. Black-breasted Blue W.

Drawn from Nature by A.Wilson

Engraved by A.Lawson

1 American Sparrow Hawk. 2 Field Sparrow. 3 Tree Sp. 4 Song Sp. 5 Chipping Sp. 6 Snow Bird.

1 *American Siskin*. 2 *Rose breasted Grosbeak*
3 *Green black throated Warbler*. 4 *Yellow rump W*. 5 *Cærulean W*. 6 *Solitary Flycatcher*.

1 Cow Bunting. 2 Female. 3 Young. 4 Maryland Yellow throat. 5 Blue grey Flycatcher. 6 White eyed F.

Drawn from Nature by A. Wilson.   Engraved by A. Lawson.

1. Red Owl   2 Warbling Flycatcher.   3. Purple Finch.   4. Brown Lark.

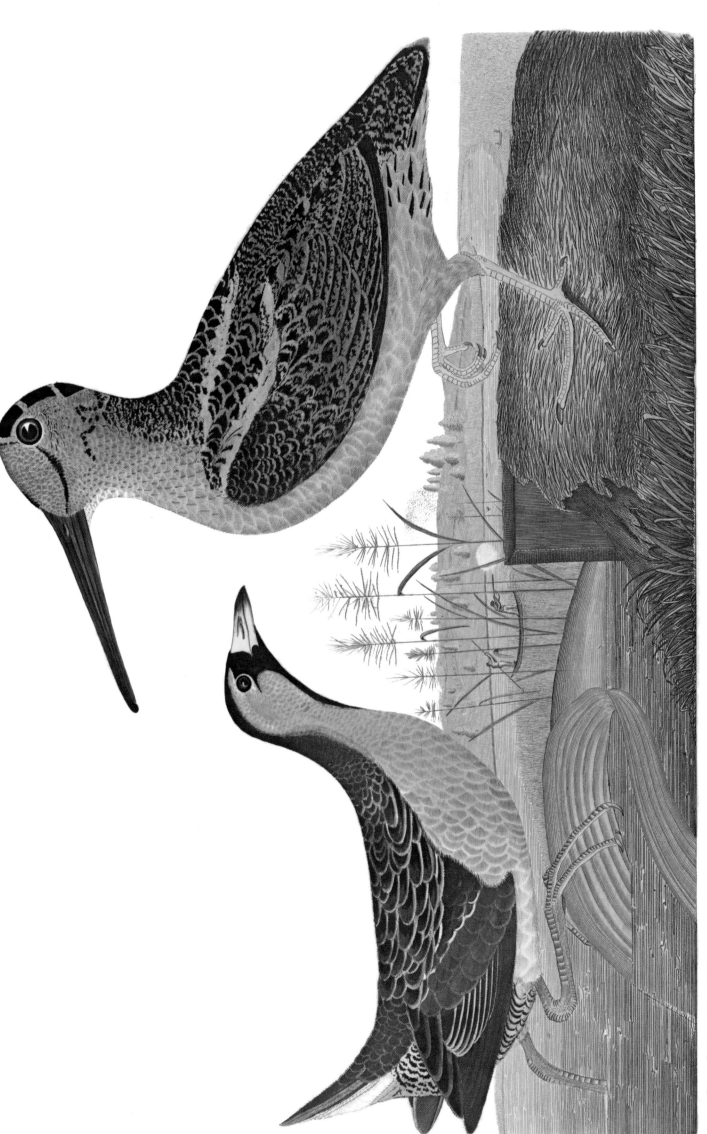

Wood Cock.

Rail.

1. *Turdus Melodus*, Wood Thrush. 2. *Turdus Migratorius*, Red-breasted Thrush, or Robin.

3. *Sitta Carolinensis*, White breasted black-capped Nuthatch. 4. *Sitta Varia*, Red-bellied-black-capped Nuthatch.

Drawn from Nature by A. Wilson.   Engraved by A. Lawson.

1. Belted Kingsfisher. 2. Black and yellow Warbler.
3. Blackburnian W. 4. Autumnal W. 5. Water Thrush.

1 Cooper's Hank
Falco Cooperii

2 Palm Warbler
Sylvia Palmarum

Drawn from Nature by A. Rider.

Engraved by Alexander Lawson.

Sharp-tailed Grous.   Tetrao Phasianellus.

Drawn from Nature by A. Wilson.   1. Virginian Rail.   2. Clapper R.   3. Blue Crane.   4. Little Egret.   Engraved by A. Lawson.

Wild Turkey, Male and Female.

Meleagris Gallopavo.

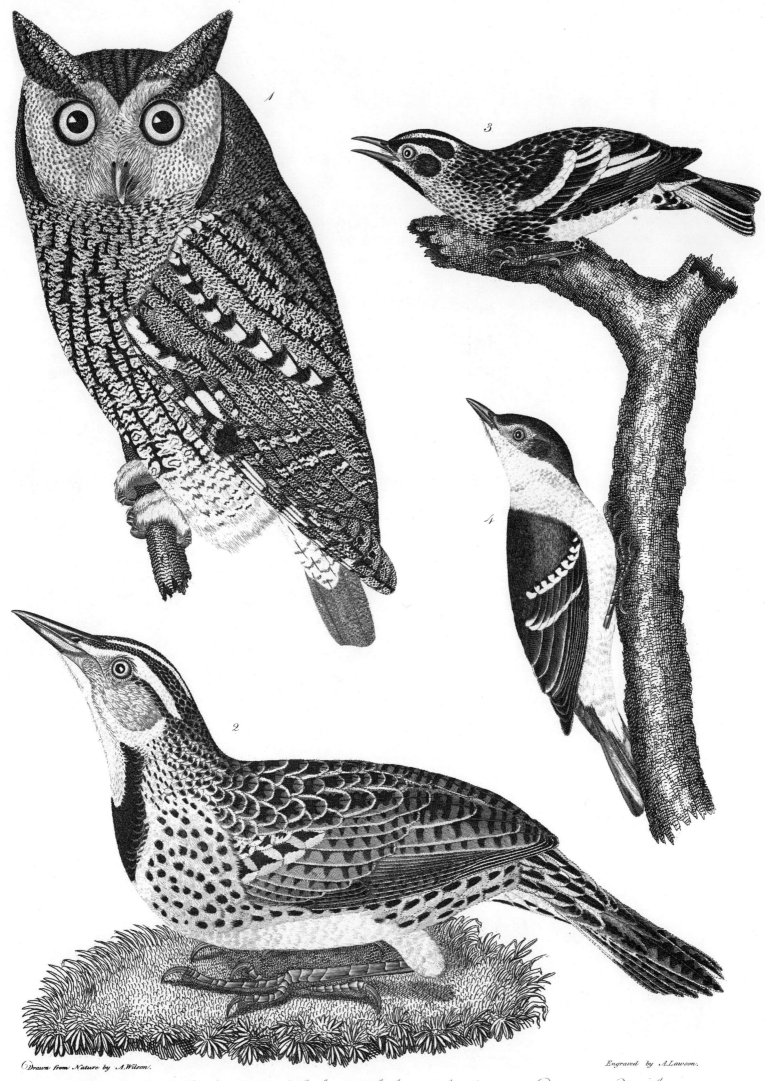

Drawn from Nature by A. Wilson.

Engraved by A. Lawson.

1. Mottled Owl. 2. Meadow Lark. 3. Black and white Creeper. 4. Pine-creeping Warbler.

Drawn from Nature by A. Wilson.

Engraved by A.Lawson.

1. Louisiana Tanager. 2. Clarks Crow. 3. Lewis's Woodpecker.

20

Drawn from Nature by A.Wilson.

Engraved by A.Lawson.

1 Canada Jay. 2 Snow Bunting. 3 Rusty Grakle. 4 Purple Grakle.

1. *Swamp Sparrow.* 2. *White-throated Sp.* 3. *Savannah Sp.* 4. *Fox-coloured Sp.* 5. *Loggerhead Shrike.*

1. Belted Kingsfisher. 2. Black and yellow Warbler.
3. Blackburnian W. 4. Autumnal W. 5. Water Thrush.

23

1. Painted Bunting 2. Female 3. Prothonotary Warbler.
4. Wormeating W. 5. Yellow-winged Sparrow. 6. Blue Grosbeak.

1.Missisippi Kite.   2.Tennesee Warbler. 3.Kentucky W. 4.Prairie W.

Drawn from Nature by A.Wilson.　　　　　　　　　　　　　　　*Engraved by A.Lawson.*

1. Carolina Parrot. 2. Canada Flycatcher. 3. Hooded F. 4. Green, black-capt F.

Drawn from Nature by A. Wilson.

Engraved by A. Lawson.

1. Pinnated Grous. 2. Blue-green Warbler. 3. Nashville W.

Drawn from Nature by A. Wilson.

Engraved by A. Lawson.

1. Carolina Cuckoo. 2. Black-billed C. 3. Blue Yellow-backed Warbler. 4. Yellow Red-poll W.

Head of the Pileated Woodpecker. size of life.

Head of the Ivory billed Woodpecker. size of life.

1. Ivory billed Woodpecker, reduced.
2. Pileated W. reduced.

3. Red headed W. drawn by the same scale.

Engraved by A. Lawson.

Drawn from Nature by A. Wilson.

29

1. Red-winged Starling. 2. Female. 3. Black-poll Warbler. 4. Lesser Red-poll.

30

Drawn from Nature by A. Wilson.

Engraved by A. Lawson.

1. American Crossbill. 2. Female. 3. White-winged Crossbill. 4. White-crown'd Bunting. 5. Bay-winged B.

31

Drawn from Nature by A. Wilson.

1. *Snow Owl.*   2. *Male Sparrow-Hawk.*

Engraved by B. Tanner.

Drawn from Nature by A. Wilson.

Engraved by A. Lawson.

1. Rough-legged Falcon. 2 Barred Owl. 3. Short-eared O.

33

Drawn from Nature by A. Wilson.　　　　　　　　　　　　　　　　*Engraved by A. Lawson.*

1. Little Owl. 2. Seaside Finch 3. Sharp-tailed F. 4. Savannah F.

Drawn from Nature by A. Wilson. 1. Winter Falcon. 2. Magpie. 3. Crow. *Engraved by A. Lawson.*

White-headed Eagle.

36

1 Fish Hawk. 2 Fish Crow. 3 Ring Plover. 4 Least Snipe.

Drawn from Nature by A. Wilson.

Engraved by J. Warnicke.

1. Barn Swallow. 2. Female. 3. White-bellied S. 4. Bank S.

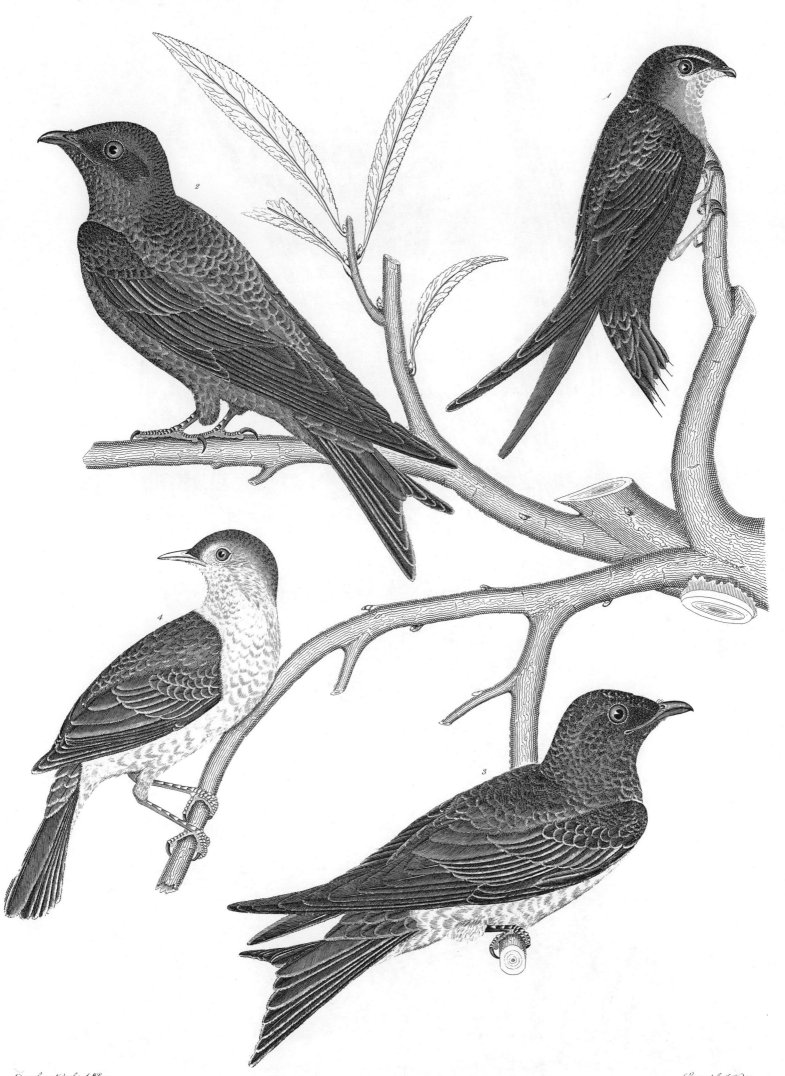

1. Chimney Swallow. 2. Purple Martin. 3. Female. 4. Connecticut Warbler.

Drawn from Nature by A. Wilson.   *Engraved by J. G. Warnicke.*

1. Night-Hawk. 2. Female.

40

Drawn from Nature by A. Wilson. *Engraved by J. G. Warnicke.*

1. Whip-poor-will 2. Female.

Drawn from Nature by A. Wilson. Engraved, by A. Lawson.

1. Red Owl. 2. Warbling Flycatcher. 3. Purple Finch. 4. Brown Lark.

Drawn from Nature by A. Wilson.   *Engraved by A. Lawson.*

1. Turtle Dove. 2. Hermit Thrush. 3. Tawney Thrush. 4. Pine-swamp Warbler.

1. Passenger Pigeon; 2. Blue-mountain Warbler; 3. Hemlock W.?

44

Drawn from Nature by A. Wilson.   *Engraved by A. Lawson.*

1. Sharp-shinnd Hawk. 2. Redstart. 3. Yellow-rump.

45

Drawn from Nature by A. Wilson. *Engraved by A. Lawson.*

1 Slate-coloured Hawk. 2 Ground Dove. 3 Female.

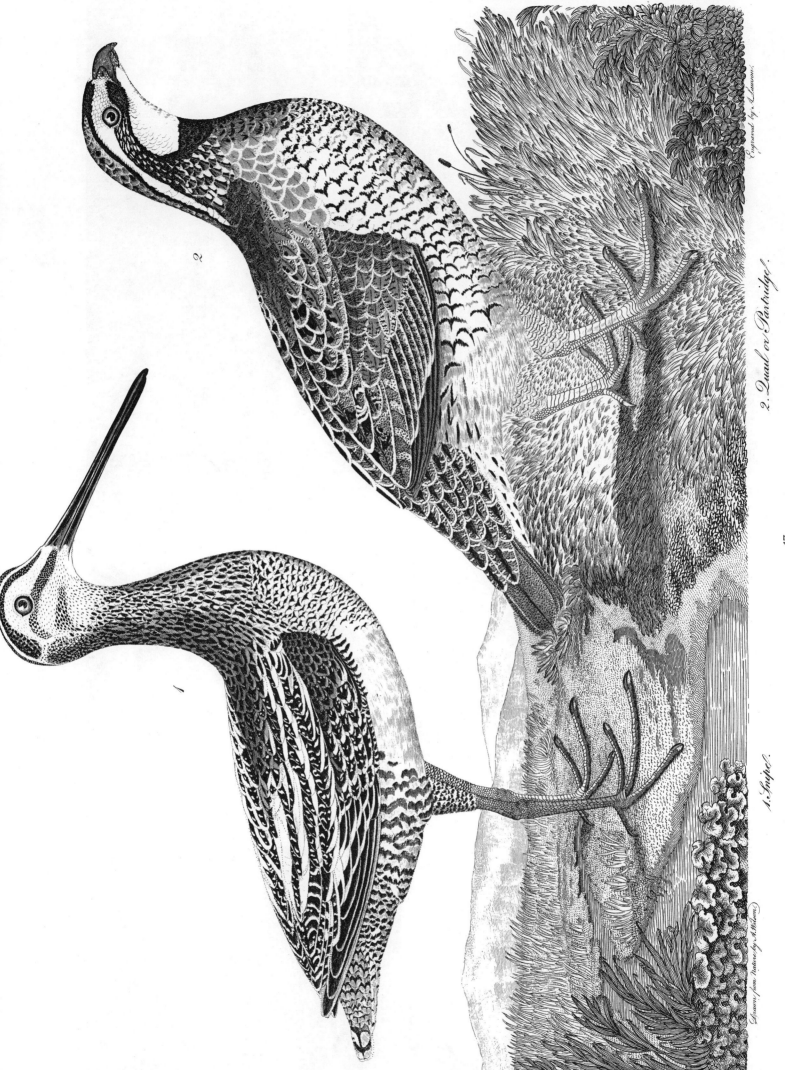

Drawn from Nature by A. Wilson.

1. Snipe.

2. Quail or Partridge.

Engraved by J. Lawson.

47

Rail.

Wood Cock.

48

Ruffed Grous or Pheasant

49

Engraved by Warnicke

Drawn from Nature by A. Wilson

Drawn from nature by A. Wilson.　　　　　　　　　　　　　　*Engraved by A. Lawson.*

1 Great Horned Owl. 2 Barn O. 3 Meadow Mouse. 4 Red Bat. 5 Small-headed Flycatcher. 6 Hawk Owl.

1 Long-eared Owl. 2 Marsh Hawk.
3 Swallow-tailed Hawk.

Drawn from Nature by A. Wilson.   Engraved by A. Lawson.

1. Red-tailed Hawk. 2. American Buzzard. 3. Ash-coloured Hawk.

Drawn from Nature by A. Wilson.

Engraved by I. G. Warnicke.

1. Black Hawk. 2. Variety of d.º 3. Red-shouldered H. 4. Female Baltimore Oriole. 5. Female Towhee Bunting.

Drawn from Nature by A.Wilson.   Engraved by I.G.Warnicke

1. Broad-winged Hawk.   2. Chuck-wills-widow.   3. Cape-May Warbler.   4. Female Black-cap W.

Drawn from Nature by A.Wilson.

Engraved by I.G.Warnicke.

1. *Ring-tail Eagle.*   2. *Sea Eagle.*

Drawn from Nature by A. Wilson. Engraved by Lawson.

1. Esquimaux Curlew.   2. Red-backed Snipe.   3. Semipalmated S.   4. Marbled Godwit.

56

Drawn from Nature by A. Wilson.   Engraved by A. Lawson.

1. Turnstone.   2. Ash-coloured Sandpiper.   3. The Purre.   4. Black-bellied Plover.   5. Red-breasted Sandpiper.

57

Drawn from Nature by A. Wilson.

Engraved by A. Lawson.

1. Red-breasted Snipe.   2. Long-legged Avoset.   3. Solitary Sandpiper.   4. Yellow-Shanks Snipe.   5. Tell-tale Snipe.

58

Drawn from Nature by A. Rider.   Engraved by I.G. Warnick.

1. Spotted Sandpiper.   2. Bartram's S.   3. Ring Plover.   4. Sanderling P.   5. Golden P.   6. Killdeer P.

Drawn from Nature by A. Wilson.   Engraved by A. Lawson.

1. Great Tern.   2. Lesser T.   3. Short-tailed T.   4. Black Skimmer.   6. Stormy Petrel.

60

1. Green Heron.   2. Night H.   3. Young.   4. Great White H.

Drawn from Nature by A. Wilson.   Engraved by J.G. Warnicke.

1. Virginian Rail.   2. Clapper R.   3. Blue Crane.   4. Little Egret.

62

1.*Roseate Spoonbill.*   2.*American Avoset.*   3.*Ruddy Plover.*   4.*Semipalmated Sandpiper.*

Drawn from Nature by A.Wilson.
Engraved by A.Lawson.

1. Lousiana Heron.   2. Pied Oyster catcher.   3 Hooping Crane.   4. Long billed Curlew.

Drawn from Nature by A. Wilson.   Engraved by I. G. Warnicke.

1. Yellow-crowned Heron.   2. Great Heron.   3. American Bittern.   4. Least B.

1. Black or Surf Duck. 2. Buffel-headed D. 3. Female. 4. Canada Goose. 5. Tufted Duck. 6. Golden-eye. 7. Shoveller.

Drawn from Nature by A. Wilson.   Engraved by G. Lawson.

1. Goosander.   2. Female.   3. Pin-tail Duck.   4. Blue-wing Teal.   5. Snow Goose.

68

Drawn from Nature by A. Wilson. Engraved by G. Warnick.

69

6 Pied Duck. 2 Red-breasted Merganser. 4 American Widgeon Male. 5 Female Snow Goose. 3 Blue Bill, or Scaup Duck. 1 Hooded, or Crested Merganser.

Drawn from Nature by A. Wilson. Engraved by Lawson.

1. Long-tailed Duck. 2. Female. 3. Summer D. 4. Green-winged Teal. 5. Canvas-back D. 6. Red-headed D. 7. Mallard.

70

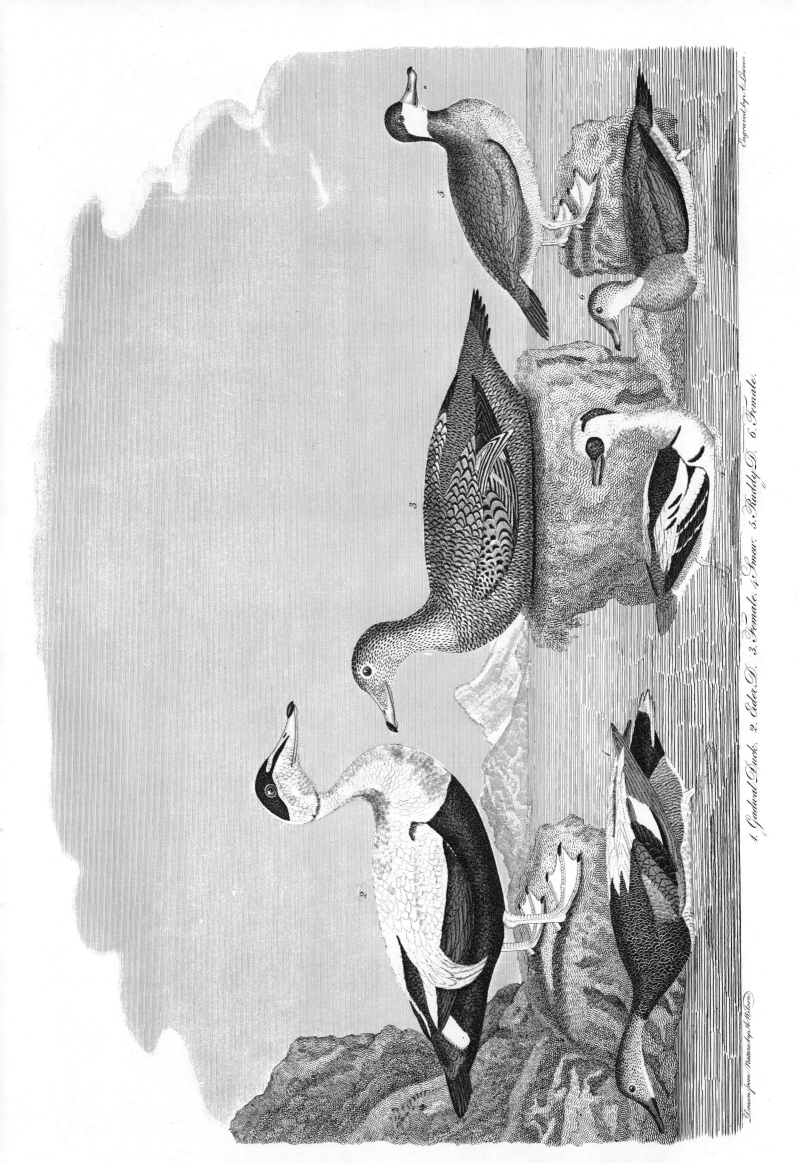

Drawn from Nature by A. Wilson.

1. Garland Duck. 2. Eider D. 3. Female. 4. Smew. 5. Ruddy D. 6. Female.

Engraved by A. Lawson.

71

Drawn from Nature by A. Wilson.   Engraved by J. Lawson.

1. Brant.   2. Scoter Duck.   3. Velvet D.   4. Harlequin D.   5. Dusky D.   6. Marsh Tern.   7. Sooty T.

Drawn from Nature by A. Wilson.   Engraved by A. Lawson.

1. Common Coot.   2 Purple Gallinule.   3. Gray Phalarope.   4. Red Phalarope.   5. Wilsons Plover.

Drawn from Nature by A. Wilson.　　　Engraved by I. G. Warnick.

1. Black-bellied Darter.　　2. Female D.　　3. Great Northern Diver.　　4. Black-headed Gull.　　5. Little Auk.

74

Head of Turkey Buzzard, size of Life.

Head of Black Vulture, size of Life.

Drawn from Nature by A.Wilson.

Engraved by A.Lawson.

1. Turkey Buzzard. 2. Black Vulture. 3. Raven.

Drawn from Nature by A. Wilson.

Great-Footed Hawk.

Engraved by A. Lawson.

76

Drawn from Nature by Titian R. Peale.   *Engraved by Alexander Lawson.*

1. Fork-tailed Flycatcher.   *2. Rocky Mountain Anteater.*   *3. Female Golden-winged Warbler.*
Muscicapa Savana.   *Myiothera Obsoleta.*   *Sylvia Chrysoptera.*

B1

1.
Swallow tailed Flycatcher.
Muscicapa Forficata.

2.
Arkansaw Flycatcher.
Muscicapa Verticalis.

3.
Say's Flycatcher.
Muscicapa Saya.

4.
Female Golden crested Wren.
Regulus Cristatus.

B2

1. *Yellow-headed Blackbird.*
Icterus Icterocephalus.

2. *Female.*

3. *Female Cape May Warbler.*
Sylvia Maritima.

1. Great Crow Blackbird. 2. Female.

Quiscalus Major.

Drawn from Nature by John J. Audubon M.R.Rides.

Engraved by Alexander Lawson.

Drawn from Nature by Titian R. Peale.

Engraved by Alexander Lawson.

1. Female Crow Blackbird.

2. Orange-crowned Warbler.

3. Lark Finch.

Quiscalus Versicolor.

Sylvia Celata.

Fringilla Grammaca.

1. Crimson-necked Bullfinch.   2. Female.   3. Arkansaw Siskin.   4. Female American Goldfinch.   5. Lazuli Finch.

Pyrrhula Frontalis.   Fringilla Psaltria.   Fringilla Tristis.   Fringilla Amoena.

Drawn from Nature by Titian R. Peale.

1. *Fulvous or Cliff Swallow.*   2. *Burrowing Owl.*
Hirundo Fulva.   *Strix Cunicularia.*

Engraved by Alexander Lawson.

Drawn from Nature by Titian R. Peale.

Engraved by Alexander Lawson.

1. and 2. *Young Yellow-bellied Woodpeckers.*　3. *Band-tailed Pigeon.*

Picus Varius.　　　*Columba Fasciata.*

B8

Drawn from Nature by Titian R. Peale.

Engraved by Alexander Lawson.

Wild Turkey, Male and Female.

Meleagris Gallopavo.

B9

1 Cooper's Hawk
Falco Cooperii

2 Palm Warbler
Sylvia Palmarum

Drawn from Nature by A. Rider

Engraved by Alexander Lawson

B10

Drawn from Nature by R. Rider.

Engraved by Alexander Lawson.

1. White-tailed Hawk.
Falco Dispar.

2. Female Cerulean Warbler.
Sylvia Azurea.

B11

Blue Hawk or Hen Harrier. B12 *Falco Cyaneus.*

Drawn from Nature by A. Rider.

Engraved by Alexander Lawson.

Drawn from Nature by A. Rider.

Engraved by Alexander Lawson.

1. *Steller's Jay.*   2. *Lapland Longspur.* 3. *Female.*
   Garrulus Stelleri.   *Emberiza Lapponica.*

Drawn from Nature by A. Rider.

Engraved by Alexander Lawson.

1. *Florida Jay.*
Garrulus Floridanus.

2. *Northern Three-toed Woodpecker.*
Picus Tridactylus.

3. *Young Red-headed Woodpecker.*
Picus Erythrocephalus.

2

3

1

4

Drawn from Nature by A. Rider.   *Engraved by Alexander Lawson.*

1   2   3   4
Evening Grosbeak.   *Female Rose-breasted Grosbeak.*   *Female White-winged Crossbill.*   *Female Indigo Finch.*

Fringilla Vespertina.   *Fringilla Ludoviciana.*   *Loxia Leucoptera.*   *Fringilla Cyanea.*

B15

1. *Pallas Dipper.*   2. *Bohemian Waxwing.*   3. *Female Pine Bullfinch.*
Cinclus Pallasii.   *Bombycilla Garrula.*   *Pyrrhula Enucleator.*

Drawn from Nature by A. Rider   *Engraved by Alexander Lawson*

1. *White-crowned Pigeon.*   2. *Zenaida Dove.*

Columba Leucocephala.   *Columba Zenaida.*

Sharp-tailed Grous. B19 Tetrao Phasianellus

Drawn from Nature by A. Rider.

Engraved by Alexander Lawson.

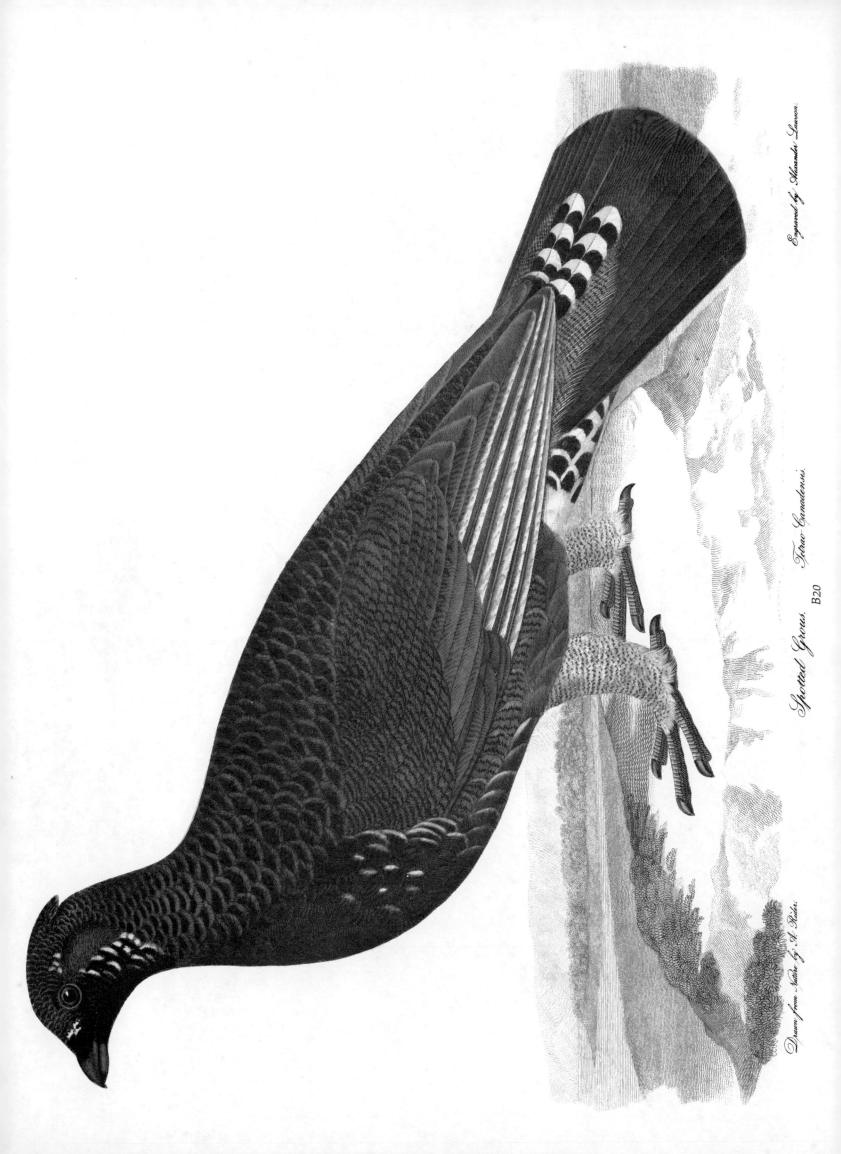

Drawn from Nature by A. Rider.

Engraved by Alexander Lawson.

1. Cock of the Plains, Female. 2. Female Spotted Grous.
Tetrao Urophasianus. Tetrao Canadensis.

B21

Young Male Condor.
Cathartes Gryphus.

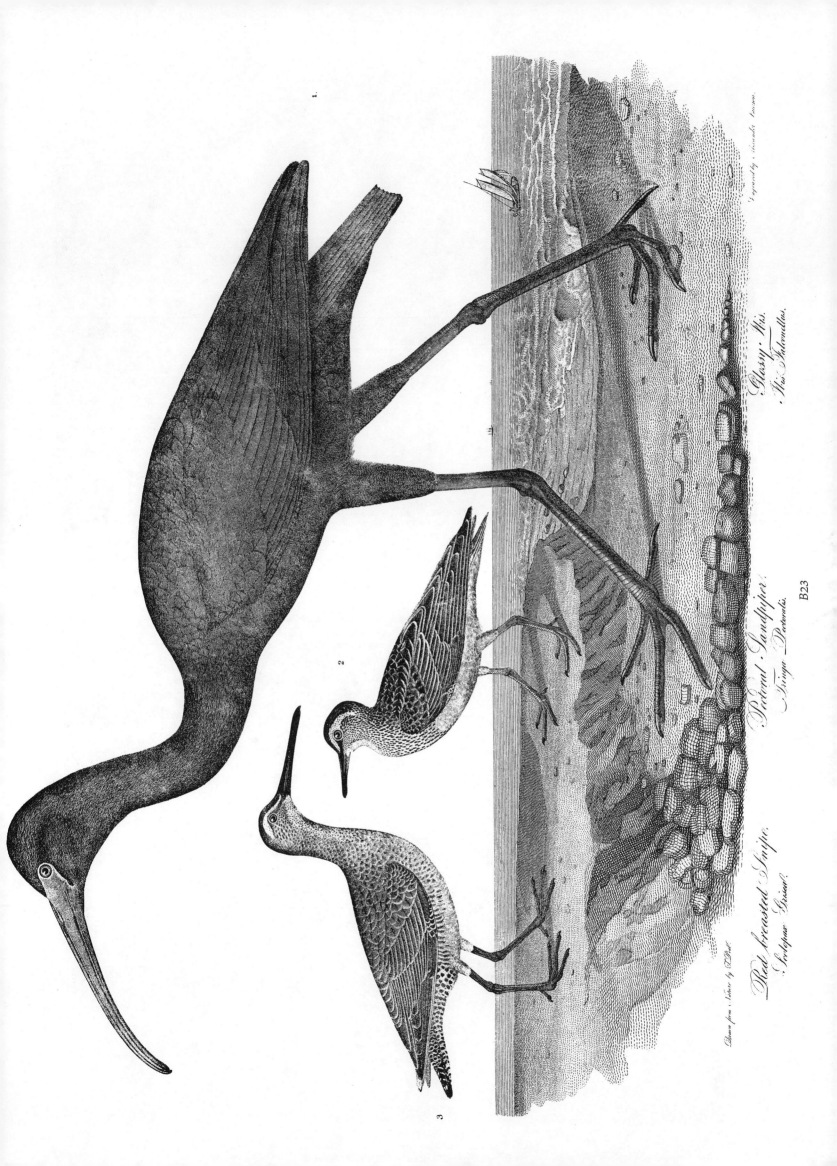

Drawn from Nature by T. Peal.

Engraved by A. Lawson. Phil.

Red breasted Snipe.
Scolopax Grisea.

Pectoral Sandpiper.
Tringa Pectoralis.

Glossy Ibis.
Ibis Falcinellus.

B23

Wilsons Phalarope.
Phalaropus Wilsonii.

Piping Plover.
Charadrius Melodus.
B24

Hinns Sandpiper.
Tringa Schinzii.

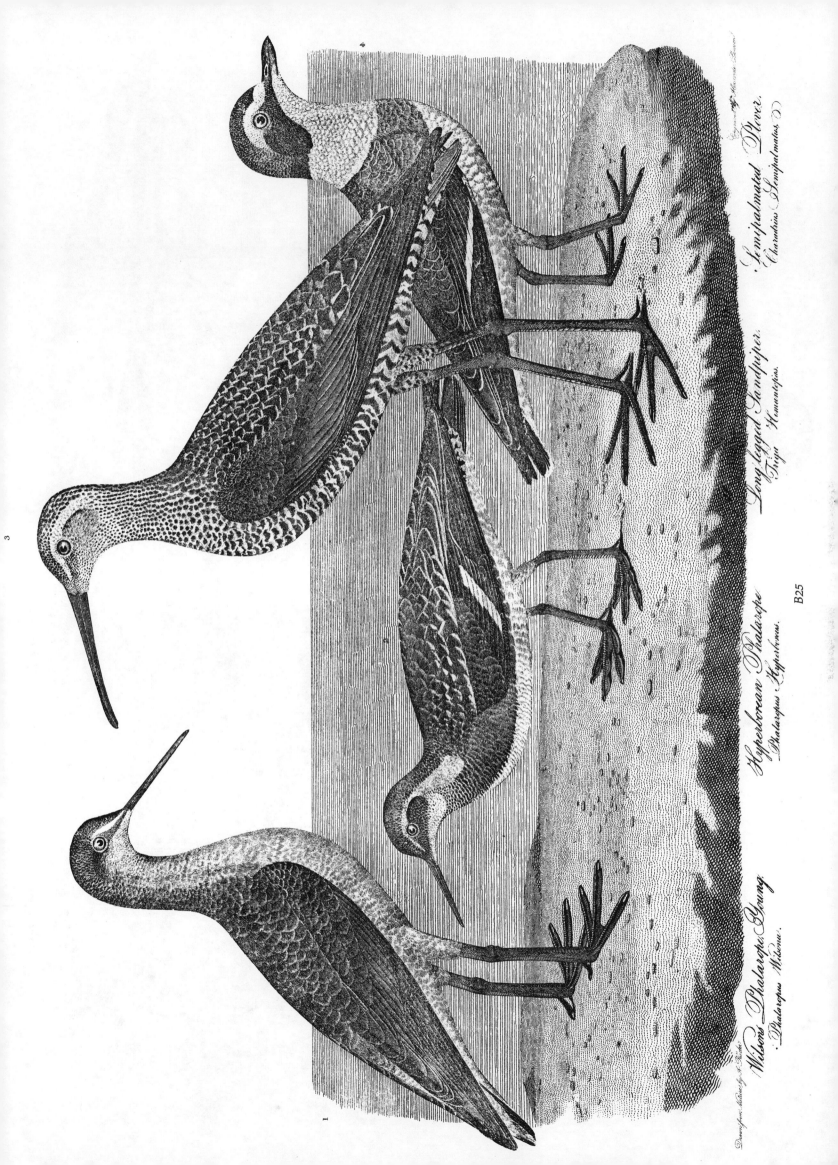

Wilsons Phalarope. Young.
Phalaropus Wilsonii.

Hyperborean Phalarope.
Phalaropus Hyperboreus.

Longlegged Sandpiper.
Tringa Himantopus.

Semipalmated Plover.
Charadrius Semipalmatus.

B25

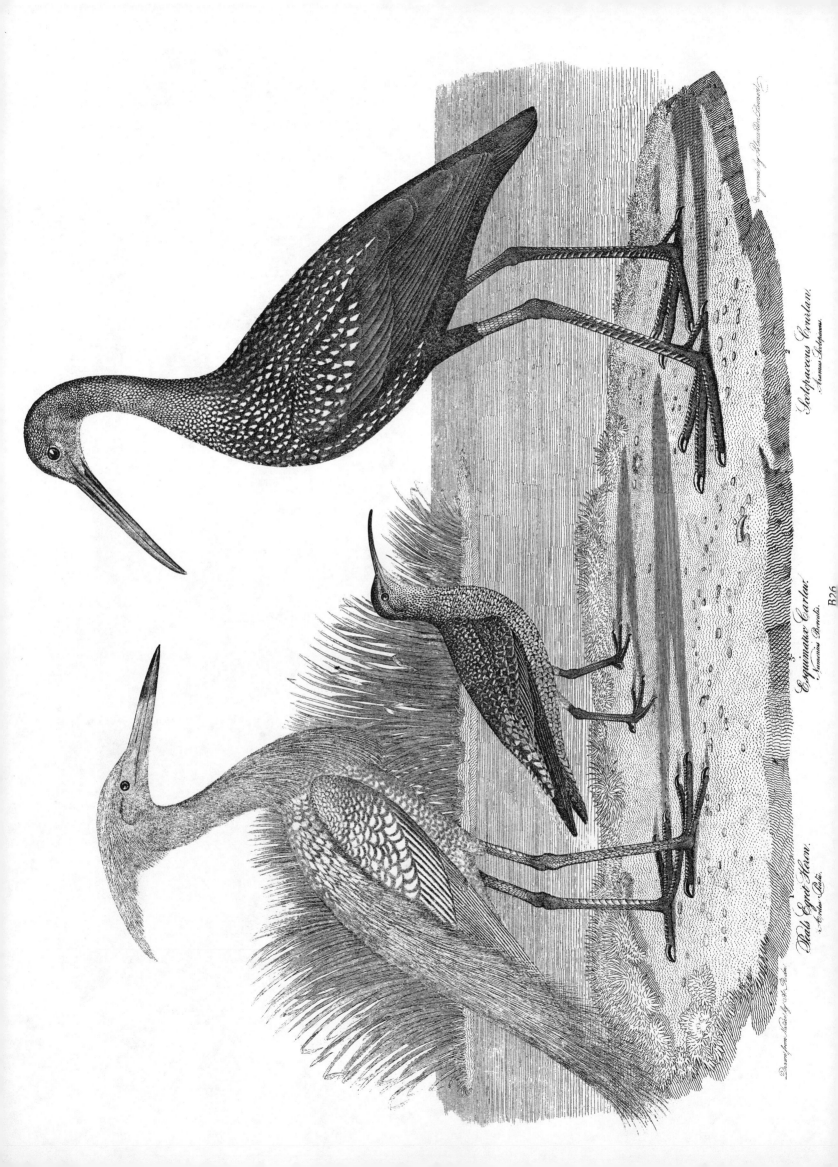

Red Egret Heron.
Ardea Rufa.

Esquimaux Curlew.
Numenius Borealis.

Scolopaceus Courlan.
Rallus Scolopaceus.

B26

Drawn from Nature by A. Rider.   *Florida Gallinule.*   ¹   *Yellow breasted Rail.*   Engraved by Alexander Lawson.
Gallinula galeata.   *Rallus noveboracensis.*

B27

INDEX OF BIRDS ILLUSTRATED

In the following index, the reader can locate a bird on the plates by looking up either its modern common name or its obsolete common name—that is, the name that actually appears on a plate. An obsolete name is always cross-referenced to the entry under the proper current name, except where it would be adjacent to the current name in the alphabetical listing. Under the current common name the reader will also find the current Latin nomenclature, the obsolete name (in parentheses) and the plate number for the bird in question.

The letter "B" preceding a plate number signifies that the plate is one of those in Bonaparte's supplement to Wilson's *American Ornithology* (see Bibliographical Note).

The following two birds are no longer recognized as valid species. They are therefore listed here only in Wilson's English and Latin nomenclature.